This Page Left Intentionally Blank

## Story 1:  My Sister Was 6

My only sister, Kiyoko, was 6 years old when I was born.  My brother, Shu, was born when she was 4 years old, but (my mother told me years later) she wanted a little sister to play with.  And we sure played together a lot.

My favorite thing to do was playing with dolls. They were paper dolls.  We cut kimonos out of Japanese paper called Chiyogami.  They were very pretty with colored pictures of flowers, birds, etc.

物語1　着せ替え人形
　　たった一人の姉きよ子さんが、6才の時に私が生まれま
した。彼女が4才の時に、私のすぐ上の兄修さんが生まれま
したが、彼女は一緒に遊べる妹が欲しかったそうです。（後
年母がそう言っていました。）その望みの通り、私達はしょ
っちゅう一緒に遊びました。
　　私の大好きな遊びは、着せ替え人形。千代紙を切り取っ
て、着物を作りました。千代紙は、きれいな鳥や花などが描
かれた、美しい色の物でした。

We also cut out a few dolls' heads with a white paper. We colored hair and drew smiling faces on them. We stuck a head into the collar (neck) of a kimono. There, a doll is born! You are able to change the dolls' kimonos so quickly. You just need to put that head into another kimono. It was like girls playing Barbie dolls here in America.

I especially liked red, pink, purple, and yellow kimonos. I felt as if I was wearing a beautiful kimono when I was playing dolls.

*Chiyogami--Origami is a well-known paper folding art. Origami papers are cut into squares. Chiyogami papers have many beautiful (mainly Japanese-kind) pictures. They are bigger than regular Origami papers and rectangular-shaped. Chiyogami papers can be used for Origami by cutting them into squares.

白い紙で人形の頭部を切り取り、髪を染めて、えがおを描き入れました。その頭部を着物の襟に入れると、1つの人形が出来上がりました。又、その頭部を別の着物の襟にさし入れるだけで、その人形はあっという間に着替えが出来ました。アメリカでも女の子達は、バービードールと言われる人形で、ドレスなどの着替えを楽しみます。

　私は特に、赤桃紫黄色の着物が好きでした。着せ替え人形で遊んでいた時には、まるで私が、それらの美しい着物を着ていたような感じに満たされたものでした。


*千代紙について ... 折り紙は、良く知られた（日本の）手芸です。紙は4角に切られています。千代紙には、美しい（日本的な）絵が付いています。それは、折り紙より大きかったり、長方形であったりします。千代紙を4角に切って折り紙にすることもできます。

## Story 2:  Bicycle Ride

My family's house was (and still is) located on a back street away from the main street in the area. There was little traffic back there then like bicycles, buggies pulled by small engines, and walking people.  Those days, only one of two town doctors had a car with a chauffeur to make house calls. Life was slow and easy, you might say.

物語2　自転車乗り

　　私の実家は、本通りから分れた裏通りにありました（今
も）。私が育つ頃は、そこは人通りが少なくて、自転車、耕
耘機で引かれたリヤカー、そして歩く人が時たま見られる位
でした。当時は町医者の1人が、おかかえの運転手で、患者
を家に診に行くための車を持っていた位でした。ゆっくりと
した時代であったと言えます。

My sister used to ride her bicycle after school or on weekends and gave me a ride on its back seat. She was always big and strong when I was a little child. The grade school playground where we used to go play was about 4-5 minutes away from our house.

Every time when we were coming back home and got to this one spot, she said to me, "Push!" while both of us were still on the bicycle. The road was slightly sloped upward and narrow but straight in a bamboo-fenced wood. One small tree root was exposed across the road, too. So, I pushed her with my body against her back while I was wrapping my arms around her waist. I just wanted to help her. I realized when I got a little older that my sister was pedaling the bicycle with the same load and weight, me, as a passenger. After that, we still continued to ride together the same way a few more years, and I "helped" her the same way but with both of us laughing every time.

姉は、放課後や週末に、私を自転車の後ろに乗せて走ったものです。私は小さい頃、彼女がいつも大きくて強いと思いました。よく遊びに行った小学校の庭は、家から4,5分の所に在りました。

　いつも帰り道に、ある一点に来ると、私達2人共自転車に乗っているのに、彼女が、「押して」と私に言いました。その通りは、少しだけ上り坂になっている竹の垣根の付いた、林の中の真っすぐな細道でした。木の根っこが、小さいけれども横切って出てもいました。私は姉の腰に手を回してつかまりながら、体を押しつけるように押しました。ただ彼女を手助けしたい一心でした。私が少し大きくなって気が付いたのは、姉は私という同じ荷物を積んだまま自転車をこいでいて、重さは変わっていなかったということです。それでも、以後も私は同じように乗ったまま、姉を押して助けました。その頃は2人共、いつもわらいながらではあったけれども。

## Story 3:  To Catch Cicadas

To catch cicadas, there was a trick.  Brother Shu and I used to make a circle with a stiff wire. We stuck it into the end of a long, bamboo stick. We wrapped the circle with very sticky spider webs (deadly for insects).  We usually found them behind sheds where there wasn't much human traffic.

物語3 せみ捕り

　　せみを捕るには、こつが必要でした。すぐ上の兄修さん
と私は、固めの針金で輪を作り、長い竹ざおの先にそれを付
けました。それに粘り気の強いクモの巣(昆虫にとっては致命
的な)を巻き付けました。それは、倉や納屋の裏など、人通
りの少ないあたりにけっこう有りました。

Then we sneaked to the tree where the cicada was singing (chirping). They usually fly upward when they fly away from us. So, you put your circle of web above the cicada then quickly bring it down to catch it. We put them in our handheld, bamboo cage to keep and look at them for a few days as if we were studying about them.

There were a few different kinds. The ones that sang in monotone on hot, summer days were Abura (oil) Zemis (cicadas). They were tough-looking with grayish-black bodies. Kanakana Zemis were rather fragile looking with transparent, greenish-blue bodies and sang in the morning or evening when it was cooler. They sang, "Kana kana kana". Then there were Minmin Zemis which sang (almost) without rest once they started, "Min min min..." The ones we weren't able to catch were Tsukutsuku Boshis because they always sang high up in trees. They sang, "Tsukutsuku iyo-, tsukutsuku iyo-" all day.

We often found cicadas after they crawled out of the ground. We watched how they came out of their brown shells which took more than a few minutes. Somehow their backs split open, and they brought their heads out of the shells first.

そしてせみの歌っている（鳴いている）木にしのび寄りました。せみは逃げるのに普通上に飛ぶので、クモの巣の輪を上から覆うように下げます。捕ったせみを虫かごの中に入れて保ち、２、３日観察するかの如く見ました。

　　せみは数種類いました。暑い夏中単調に歌うのは、油ぜみ。彼らは、灰色っぽい黒の頑丈な感じに見える体をしています。カナカナぜみは、こわれそうな透き通るような緑がかった青の体で、朝夕の涼しい時に歌います。「カナカナカナ」と。そしてミンミンぜみは１度歌い始めると、１日中休むことも　無いかと思われる位、「ミンミンミン」と鳴き続けます。ツクツク法師は、いつも木のずうっと高い所で鳴くので、私達は１度も捕ったことがありません。かれらは１日中、「ツクツクイヨーツクツクイヨー」と鳴きます。

　　私はせみが地中から出て来て、茶色の殻から抜け出るところを何度かこの目で見たことが有ります。それは数分の事ではありません。最初に背中が半分に分かれて、頭から先に出て来ます。

Later in life, I learned that they stay down in the ground for several years then live on trees only a few weeks. They sing with their wings and bodies by vibrating -- not with their voices like human beings. I didn't know those things then. We just had fun catching them during the Summer. They sure were singing all day as if they were enjoying their short heyday.

I've often heard Abura Zemis here in Kansas on hot summer days and found empty shells, too. The other day, I saw an Abura Zemi on the stem of a big, sunflower plant in my friend's yard. I had to go see it closely. I've never seen other cicadas here, though.

後になって知ったのですが、彼らは地面の中に何年もいて、地上に出てからはほんの数週間しか生存しないということです。彼らは人間のように歌うのでなくて、羽と体を振動しながら音を出して歌うということです。私はそんなことは知りませんでした。ただ彼らを捕ることだけが楽しみでした。彼らもただ短い全盛期を満喫せんとばかりに、一生懸命歌っていました。

　私はここキャンザスで、夏の暑い日に油ぜみが鳴いているのを聞き、空っぽの殻も幾つか見ました。この間は友達の庭で、油ぜみが大きなひまわりの幹にとまっているのを見ました。私はそれを見たい一心で、近づきました。でも他の種のせみは、ここで見たことがありません。

## Story 4:   After Rice Was Harvested

After rice was harvested, my parents spread many straw mats in our yard.  They were the size of single bed mattresses.  They were woven at home by a hand-operated machine with rice straws.

My father carried newly harvested rice which were still in husks from storage, one bushel at a time, in a strong container on his shoulder.  After he dumped it on the mat, my mother spread the small mound of grain evenly thin onto the rest of the space of the mat with a wooden rake.

物語 **4** 米の収穫

　米の収穫が終わった後、私の両親はむしろを庭にたくさん敷きました。むしろはふとんの大きさ位で、機械と手を交互に使って稲のわらで織られたものでした。

　父はまだもみがらの中に入っている新米を、頑丈な容器で一杯ずつ肩にかついで、納屋から運んで来ました。それをむしろの1ヶ所に小山の様におくと、母が木の熊手でゆっくりとむしろ一杯に薄く広げました。

During the day, they went out to move kernels by gathering and spreading again with a rake. That's how each kernel was dried completely.

When they first spread the mats, my brother and I were very happy. We were like a couple of puppy dogs around my parents' feet. We did somersaults on the mats. We looked at familiar scenes upside down. I thought they looked different, and it made me feel like I was in strange places. Then we lay down on them with our arms and legs stretched out just to see the blue sky.

Then before sundown, my parents carried the grain back into the shed the same way they carried it out. The straw mats were folded and stored in the shed, also. That was only one of many things needing to be done from the time rice seeds were planted until the time the rice made it onto our table for us to eat. I saw that. That's why I couldn't waste even a small amount of rice for a long time.

A lot of farm work is done by machine now including drying grains.

日中彼らは又、それぞれのむしろの米を、それぞれかき集めては、又熊手でそれぞれに薄く広げました。米はそのようにして乾燥されました。

　そのむしろを最初に広げた時に、兄と私はとてもうれしくて、まるで子犬の様に、両親の足元をかけ回っていたものです。むしろの上で、とんぼ返りをしたり、周りの景色を逆さまに見たりしました。見慣れた光景でもそう見ると、全然知らない地に行ったような感じがしました。最後には、手足を大の字に伸ばしてむしろの上に寝ころんで、ただ青い空を見ました。

　夕方両親は又、むしろの米をそれぞれ集めて容器に入れ肩にかついで納屋に運び込みました。むしろもたたんで納屋に入れました。それは米の種が蒔かれる時から、食卓に出るまでのたくさんの過程を過ぎる、ほんの一部の労働です。私はそれをこの目でみました。それなので、私は少しの残りご飯でもすてるということが、長い間出来ませんでした。

　今は多くの農業は、穀物を乾かすのも含めて、機械でやっているようです。

## Story 5:  When There Weren't Any Supermarkets

When there weren't any supermarkets in the area where I grew up years ago, there were many specialized stores (like for food, clothing, medicine, etc.) in town.  Farmers grew most everything they ate right at home then except fish.

物語5 スーパーマーケットが無かった頃

　　私が育った地方では、スーパーマーケットが無かった頃
は、町にそれぞれの品物を売る専門屋がそれぞれに有りまし
た。たとえば乾物屋、呉服屋、薬局などです。農家では、魚
以外は、ほとんど家で作るという自給自足の生活でした。

In the Fall, it was delicious mackerel pike season, and they were plentiful. My favorite fish was large blue mackerel. A man who pulled a wooden cart behind a very sturdy bicycle came by farm houses to sell fish. Many fish were kept in crushed ice in a large box in that cart. Most farmers bought them, so they didn't have to go to town to get them. They were very fresh -- right out of the fish market. The fish market at the Pacific Ocean was about 80 km (50 miles) away from where we lived.

The guys who brought fish must have had strong muscles to pedal a bicycle with such a load. Also, the people who worked at several fish markets I have seen in the past were very lively. They were like freshly caught fish. I imagined that those men I saw years ago must have been strong and cheerful people and liked to do what they were doing.

My family always bought some fish from them. My mother cooked the fish with egg plants or cut up large radishes -- whatever was available that time of year. After that, my father always told me to have a portion closest to the tail, including the tail. He said, "Since you are the youngest."

秋はサンマの季節で、それはふんだんに有りました。私のすきな魚は、大きな青いサバでした。頑丈な自転車でリヤカーを引いた男の人が、魚を売る為に農家を１軒１軒回って来ました。リヤカーの中には、砕いた氷の中にたくさんの魚が入った大きなハコが有りました。多くの農家では、町に魚を買いに行かなくてすむので、それを買ったようです。魚は魚市場からまっすぐに運ばれて来たのでしょう、とても新鮮でした。私の住んでいたあたりは、太平洋の魚市場からは８０キロメートル位離れていました。

　　自転車をこいで、あんなに重そうな荷物を運んで来た人達は、たぶん力の有る人達だったと思います。又、私がこれまで見た魚市場で働く人達は、とても活気の有る人達ばかりでした。まるで、水の中から釣り上げたばかりのピチピチとした魚の様でした。あの頃見た魚売りの人達は、力が強くて楽観的で、その仕事が好きであったのでしょう。

　　私の家族は、いつもその人達から魚を買いました。母はその季節に豊富なナスや、ダイコンのぶつ切りなどと一緒にそれを煮ました。そして食べる段階になったら、父がいつも私に、しっぽに近い部分を食べるように言いました。「一番下なんだからナ」と。

When I look back on those days, I have to say that my parents knew what they were doing. The richly fat, chest-portion of the fish has a 3-way bone structure to encase the lungs and the guts whereas the tail portion has only a 2-way bone structure. They didn't want me to swallow bones and the bones get stuck in my throat as the chest-portion bones are thin and can be missed easily. From such a simple act, I figured that I was loved and cared for well. I never doubted that the near-tail portion, which was thin, tasted as good as the rest of the fish.

今考えてみると、両親はちゃんと知っていたのだナアと思います。油ののった胸あたりの肉は、肺と腹わたを囲む様に、ほねがせぼねから３方に出ています。しっぽに近くなると、２方にしか出ていません。その胸のあたりの肉を私が食べて、小さくて見のがしやすいほねがのどにつかえたりしないようにとの、両親の思いやりであったのでしょう。そんなささいなことにも気をくばって良くめんどうを見てくれた両親に、私はとても愛されていたと思いました。そのしっぽに近い薄っぺらな肉が、他の部分より劣っていたとは、一度も思ったことがありませんでした。

## Story 6:  My Family's Cow

My family's cow was old.  I don't remember if she even had a name.  She was kept as a farm laborer.  She pulled a buggy and pulled a plow.  My family fed her dried straw which was chopped up by a hand-operated machine and some other green plants without chopping.  She stayed in a small barn with straw for her bed and mooed when she was hungry.

物語6　家の牛

　　私の家の牛は老いていました。その牛に名前がついてい
たか、私は覚えていません。牛は馬車を引いたり、農地を耕
す為に飼われていました。私の家族は、手で押した機械で麦
わらを切った飼い葉と、切らないままの緑の草などをあたえ
ました。小さな牛小屋に、麦わらをフトンとして寝、空腹の
時には、モーモーと泣いていました。

One day the cow died. My mother was very sad. She told me how much the cow helped her with the farm work, especially when my father was away because of WWII. I always thought that the cow had very gentle eyes. She moved rather slowly, maybe because she was already old when I became aware of her existence. The people who took care of dead animals came to get her body. I have never found out what they did with it. Often, I wondered if they made shoes out of her hide.

Soon after that, many farmers started buying small engines to pull carts and cultivate farm land with. My family bought one, too. The daily chore of "feeding the cow" was not needed anymore.

I'd never eaten beef until I was in high school. My second oldest brother, Joji, was working in Tokyo then, and he took me to a Sukiyaki house. Sukiyaki is a famous Japanese dish, but people in Japan were not accustomed to eating beef until recent years. I ate beef for the first time, and it was good. I didn't think about that gentle-eyed cow, either.

ある日、その牛が死んでしまいました。私の母はとても悲しかったようでした。彼女が私に言ったことは、特に戦争中に、夫（私の父）を兵隊にとられてしまって人手不足だった時に、その牛が彼女の農業を良く手伝ってくれたということでした。私はいつも、その牛が優しい目をしていたと思いました。そして動くのもゆっくりと（急に動かず、子供を驚きこわがらせることも無く）でした。それは、私がその牛の存在を知った頃には、その牛がすでに年とっていたからかもしれません。死んだ家畜を引き取る業をしている人達が来て、その死体を持ち去って行きましたが、それをどうしたかは、私は知りません。その皮でクツでも造ったかもしれないと思ったりしました。

　その頃、近所の農家では耕耘機を買うようになり、リヤカーを引いたり農地を耕したりするようになりました。私の家でもそれを買い、毎朝夕牛にえさをあたえる仕事はしなくてすむようになりました。

　私は高校に入った頃まで、牛肉を食べたことが有りませんでした。当時2番目の兄丈二さんが、東京で仕事をするようになって、私をスキヤキ屋に連れて行ってくれました。スキヤキは日本の代表的な料理として世界で知られていますが、日本人は昔は牛を食べていなかったようです。私はその時初めて牛肉を食べ、それはおいしいと思いました。そしてあの優しい目の牛のことも思わずに。

## Story 7:  When I First Saw The Pacific Ocean

When I first saw the Pacific Ocean, I was 11 years old.  The previous year, all the 4$^{th}$ graders went to Tokyo Bay to dig shell fish.  We dug plenty of shells in the tide-ebbed sand and didn't see much water.

物語7 初めて太平洋を見た時のこと
　　私が初めて太平洋を見たのは、１１才の時でした。その前の年に４年生全員が、東京湾（稲毛海岸）に潮干狩りに行きました。干潮の砂浜で、貝をたくさん掘ることが出来ましたが、海水は見えませんでした。

The time when water moved in because of the changing tide, we were told to hurry back on the shore. So, I didn't see the real ocean nor smell it.

Those days, many farmer families didn't have extra cash. So, they didn't encourage their children to explore outside of their area. Out of 120 classmates, only a quarter of them went on this trip. My parents thought that it might be an educational experience for me to go. So, they paid for me.

The Pacific Ocean was wide open at the spot where we were. Huge waves continuously came crashing into the big rocks in some rocky areas. The sandy beach was comfortable for our bare feet. And the smell of the ocean air was so cool that there was nothing I could compare it with.

We stood on the sandy shore in small groups. Our teacher told us to hold each other's hands and walk toward the sea. "Jump when you see the wave," the teacher said. We all started walking; our knees then chests went in the cold seawater. Then, we met a huge wave. So, we tried to jump, but we were too short. The wave swallowed us and went above our heads. I didn't hold anyone's hands then. I couldn't.

満ち潮になる為海水がじりじりと増えて来た時には、私達はさっさと岸に引き上げる様に言われたので、波も見ず、そのにおいというものをかぐことも出来ませんでした。

あの頃は、農家では現金という物は、あまり余分に無い家が多かったようです。それで子供達に対して、他の地を知ってこいという勧めが少なかったようです。１２０人もの級友の中で、今回の旅に行くことが出来たのは、ほんの４分の１位でした。私の両親は、教育の為になるだろうと、私の為に旅費を払ってくれました。

私達が行った太平洋岸は、全く広々とした所でした。大波が大きな岩に当たり砕けては又次の大波が来て砕けて、終止すること無く打っていました。砂浜は、はだしで歩くのにとても気持ちの良い所でした。そして海のにおいはすがすがしく、他に例える物が有りませんでした。

私達は、皆一緒に砂浜に立ちました。先生が皆んなでお互い手をとって、横に１列になって海に向かって歩きましょうと言い、「波が来たらジャンプしましょう」とも言いました。それで、皆んなで手を取って歩き始め、最初はひざ、次に胸のあたりまで、冷たい海水につかりました。そうしたら、大波が来たのでジャンプしましたが、私達は背がひくすぎたようです。その波は私達をのみ込んで、頭の上を通り越して行きました。私は誰の手も握っているどころではありませんでした。

I didn't think anybody else was capable of holding hands, either. My body was upside down then turned sideways. I was rolling in the water. By the time I was able to stand on my feet, I had swallowed a lot of water. I heard that the ocean water was salty, but "I didn't know THIS salty," I thought. I don't remember how we spent the rest of the day, but I can't forget that I did somersaults in that big wave that day.

Every time when I stand at the shore of southern California and look toward Japan, I can't help thinking, "Pacific Ocean is huge!" I couldn't imagine how big it was when I first saw it, but now I know after flying over it several times.

*It takes about 10 hours from Japan to the west coast of the United States with the fastest jumbo jet which flies about 550 miles an hour.

他の子供達誰も手など握っていることは出来なかったと思います。私の体は逆さになって、次には横になって、海水の中で何度か回転したような気がします。両足で立つことが出来た時には、私は水をたくさん飲んでいました。海の水が塩からいとは聞いていましたが、「こんなにしょっぱいとは思わなかった」と思ったものです。私はそれ以後、あの日をどの様に過ごしたかは覚えていないけれども、あの大きな波の中で宙返りをしたことだけは忘れられません。

　　いつでも日本に向かって、南カリフォルニアの岸に立つ時に、「太平洋とは広大なものだ」と思わざるをえません。私がそれを初めて見た時に、いかに大きいものか想像も出来なかったけれども、何度か飛行機で往復したことの有る今、本当にその大きさを知ったと言えます。


*日本からアメリカの西海岸まで、1番速い旅客機（時速1.6キロメートルX550）で、約10時間はかかります。

## Story 8:   One Man Picture Story Show

One of the fun things during summer vacation was a one man picture story show.

The guy, sometimes young and sometimes older, rode a bicycle and came around farm communities. He had his medium-sized, wooden box full of candies on his back seat.  He parked the bicycle in the shade and made unique noises by hitting two wooden sticks together.  We all knew that it was "one man picture story show time".

物語**8** 紙芝居屋

　　夏休みの楽しみのひとつは、紙芝居屋が回って来るとい
うことでした。

　　**1**人の男の人が、時には若かったり時には中年だったり
で、自転車に乗って農家のあたりを回って行きました。自転
車の荷台には、中位の大きさの木のハコを積んで、その中に
はあめがたくさん入っていました。自転車を木陰に停めて、
拍子木を使って独特の音をたてました。それが紙芝居の始ま
る時間であることを、私達は知っていました。

When children gradually gathered, he opened the drawers of that wooden box and sold candies. They were a little different-shaped from the ones sold in stores. So, we thought that they tasted very different from the candy stores' candies. When he was done selling them, he set up the stage for his show. He put the wooden frame on top of the candy box. There were many pages of brightly-colored pictures in that frame. He read a story by looking at the back of the frame where the story must have been written. It's like a mother reading a story book for her children and showing the pictures on each page. Those days, farmers worked all day and all the time, so most mothers didn't have time to read books for their children. Well, the one man picture story show guy had to be many characters, so he changed his voice for each character. He must have had to remember which person had what kind of voice. He read loudly sometimes. When he read very quietly, we all had to listen very attentively. When the story got to the climax, often he said that it'd be continued the next day.

子供達が少しずつ集まり始めると、彼はハコの引き出しからあめを取り出して売り始めました。普通の店で売っていたあめなどと見かけが違っていたので、味もずうっと違うのかと思わせました。彼がいちおうあめを売り終えた後、芝居の舞台をしくみました。木の枠を、あめのハコの上に乗せたものです。その枠の中には、美しい色で塗り描かれた絵のページが、何枚か入っていました。物語は、その枠の裏側から読むことが出来たのでしょう、彼はそこから読んでいました。それはお母さんが子供達に絵本を読んでいるのと同じです。その頃、ほとんどの農家のお母さん達は、一日中垣間無く働いて子供達に本を読んでいる時間も有りませんでした。そして紙芝居屋は、１人で何人もの役をしなければならなかったので、役によってそれぞれ声を変えなければなりませんでした。彼はどの人がどんな声であったのかを覚えていなければならなかったでしょう。彼は時には声を張り上げ、時には静かに読んだりしました。静かに小声で読んだ時には、私達は特に耳を傾けて聞かなければなりませんでした。そして物語が、興味絶好の頂点に達した時に、続きは明日ということが、度々有りました。

I had a hard time waiting to find out the rest of the story. The next day, I made sure that I did not miss going to the same place to watch it. Those days, televisions weren't owned by most farmers yet, and we listened to stories on the radio. So, those stories with pretty, colored pictures were very exciting to us.

Before the closing, he gave us quizzes and gave those children who gave right answers one candy each. We were wanting to win candies, so we all tried to answer the questions. He folded and packed his stage onto the wooden box again and rode off to the next place. I wondered in later years where he was from. I don't know if he knew how much adults and children in the farm communities appreciated him.

私はその物語の続きを待ちきれない思いで、次の日も必ずその場に行くことに努めました。その頃は、テレビはほとんどの農家には無くて、物語はラジオで聞きました。紙芝居屋の美しく塗められた絵を見ながら聞く物語には、とても感激したものでした。

　終わりに彼は私達にクイズをあたえ、正解の出来た子達にあめをあたえるのが常でした。私達はあめが欲しくて、一生懸命それを解こうとしました。そして彼は又、その舞台をたたんで、あめのハコに縛って、自転車をこいで、次の場所にと去って行きました。後年になって私は、その人（達）がどこから来たのかと思ったことがありました。農家の大人達と子供達が、彼らにどれほど感謝していたか、彼らが知っていたかどうかは、私は知る由も有りません。

## Story 9:   A Total Sun Eclipse

A total sun eclipse happens rarely, and when it happens, it can be seen only from some parts of the Earth.

One day when I was in 3$^{rd}$ or 4$^{th}$ grade, I can't recall which, we (all of the grade school pupils) were told to go out on the playground.  We children and teachers all went out with dark, stiff, plastic sheets in our hands.  The plastic sheet was used for everyday school work when we wrote on notebook pages with a pencil.

物語9　皆既日食

　　皆既日食はめったに起こらなくて、起こってもそれは、地球のほんの一部でしか見ることが出来ません。

　　私が3年か4年の時、それははっきり覚えていませんが小学校の生徒達皆校庭に出るように言われました。生徒達と先生達皆んな、暗く固い下敷きを手に外に出ました。それは毎日の学業に、鉛筆でノートに書く時に使われた物です。

If you put it under a page before you write with a pencil, the next page would not be affected and still look new with no marks left from the previous page. It was one of the must have items for grade school children. Each one of them came in a single color but were sold in many different colors, and some light-colored ones were pretty. We needed dark ones that day.

The teacher explained to us beforehand with a picture that the sun would be covered by the moon. I had never heard such a thing until I overheard grown-ups talking about it a few days before. We waited only a short time once we got outside. Pretty soon, we noticed that shadows of round leaves were getting to be half-moon shaped, then a waning moon. It was a very strange sight. Soon, all the leaves disappeared. Nobody had a shadow from her or his body, either. We looked at the mid day sun through plastic sheets and were able to see it directly. The round moon was right over the sun as if you just put a fitting puzzle piece there. I expected all around us to be pitch-dark. But amazingly, we were able to see each other and all the objects around in light-black shades as if it was shortly after sundown.

それを下に敷いて書くと、次のページに何の跡も残らず真新しいのと同じです。それは小学生の必需品であり、それらは数々の色で売られていて、明るい色のはとてもきれいでした。その日は暗い色の物が必要でした。

　　外に出る前に私達は先生から、絵付きで、月が太陽を隠してしまうという説明を聞いていました。私はそんなことは以前聞いたことも無く、数日前に大人達が話していたのが初めてでした。外に出てあまり長く待たないうちに、丸い木の葉の影が半月形になりました。次にそれらが3ヶ月形になり、そのうちに完全に消えてしまいました。それは本当に異様な光景でした。立っている私達の影も、皆消えてしまいました。私達は下じきを通して太陽を見ました。月は太陽の中にすっぽりと入ってしまって、まるでジグソーパズルの1片が、ぴったりとはまった感じでした。私は回りが暗やみの様に真っ暗になることを期待していました。ところが驚くことに、夕方の様にまだあたりが薄暗くて、少しは周囲がわかる様な感じでした。

I saw the sun's rays leaking out from behind the fitted puzzle piece. "Wow," I said with amazement at the sun's might. "The moon couldn't hide the sun's rays," I thought. It lasted a very short time, and we were back into normal daylight again.

太陽の光が、そのぴったりとはまった1片の周囲から、もれ
ている様にわずか見えました。「わああっ」とその時私は、
太陽の強さに驚かされたものです。月は太陽を全部隠すこと
が出来なかったと。それはほんの数分間しか続かなくて、又
普通の陽に戻りました。

## Story 10:  July 7<sup>th</sup> In Japan

July 7<sup>th</sup> in Japan was a fun day for the children who lived in the countryside when I was growing up. It was Tanabata festival day.  We decorated medium-sized bamboo trees like here in America during Christmas time on evergreen trees.  On colorful, long, rectangular papers, we wrote words like "Amanogawa (Milky Way)", "Tanabata (Evening of the Seventh Month)", etc.  We wrote them with a calligraphy pen which always used homemade, black ink.

物語 10　たなばた

　　私が育つ頃の7月7日は、田舎に住む子供達にとっては
楽しい日でした。それはたなばた祭りの日でした。アメリカ
で、緑のクリスマスツリーを飾るように、どこの家でも中位
の竹を飾りました。ふでで細長い色紙に、天の川、たなばた、
七月七日などと書きました。

We tied two or three of them (one piece at a time), with short, paper strings, to each bamboo branch. The whole family admired the decorated tree for a few days by saying, "How pretty it is!" Also, little children pulled homemade, straw horses and tied them to the tree to rest.

My eldest brother, Sadao (12 years older than me), made me a horse one year. My father was making them for Brother Shu and me before that. I wonder why my father didn't make them that year? Maybe he thought we were getting too old to play with them. I was 7 or 8 years old and Brother Shu was 9 or 10. I don't remember if Brother Sadao made one for Brother Shu, but I remember that I was so happy with mine. I felt my oldest brother's gentleness then more than any other time before.

The horses were made out of rice straws. Some people used reed straws. The horses had long faces, small ears, and long necks. Those horses never had eyes, so I never thought that was strange. They had two short legs. The neck and legs were tightly tied into the body which was a bundle of straws.

それらを短い紙の糸で、ひとつひとつ、それぞれの枝に２、３枚つるしました。そしてそれを、縄で杭に縛って立てました。家族中で、それがいかに美しいかを、２、３日称え合いながら見ました。又、小さい子供達は、それぞれの家庭で作ったわらの馬をその竹の幹に縛って、馬が休んでいるという光景を作りました。

　私の１番上の兄貞雄さんは、私より１２才年上で、ある年にその馬を作ってくれました。それまでは父が毎年、私とすぐ上の兄修さんに作ってくれたような気がします。どうしてあの年、父が作らずに兄が作ってくれたのかは、記憶に残っていません。たぶん私達がその馬で遊ぶには、大きくなりすぎていたのかもしれません。私が７つか８つ、修さんは９つか１０位だったから。貞雄さんが、修さんにも作ってあげたかどうかはわかりませんが、私はとてもうれしかったことを覚えています。彼の優しさが、それ以前以上に感じられました。

　たなばたの馬は、稲わらで作られました。人によっては葦の葉を使うこともあるようです。長い顔と、小さい耳、そして長い首を持っていました。目は描かれてもなく、特別に何も付けて無かったのが普通だったので、目が無いということを不思議にも思いませんでした。そして２本の短い足が有って、首と足はわらの束が縛られた胴体に入れてありました。

And the long bundle was left uncut to make it into a long tail so the two-legged horse could stand upright. We pulled them with a rope which was made out of rice straws, also. When the horses decided to run, we had to run. We stopped at the roadside to feed them a special kind of grass which we were shown by older children in the past. When the horses turned corners, we had to go slowly so the horses didn't tip over to the side.

That was the last year I played with a straw horse. Sister Kiyoko, Brother Shu, and I decorated the bamboo tree a few more years yet with no horses to be tied to the tree to rest.

*Tanabata--The story we were told was that Prince Hikoboshi and Princess Orihime only get to meet once a year, July 7th, by the shores of the Milky Way which is Amanogawa (Sky's River) in Japanese.

そしてその束は縛られずに、切られることも無く、後ろに自由に伸ばしてあって、それがしっぽでした。その長いしっぽの為に、２本足の馬は立つことが出来ました。私達はそれを縄で引いて遊びました。馬が早く走るとなると、私達も早く走らなければなりませんでした。又えさをあたえる為、道端に停まったりもしました。えさは以前年上の子達から教わった一種の草でした。馬が角を曲がる時には、私達はゆっくりと行かなければなりませんでした。そうしなかったら、馬がわきに倒れてしまうから。

　あの年が、私がたなばたの馬と遊んだ最後でした。以後も数年、きよ子さんと修さんと私でたなばたの竹を飾り立てましたが、それに連なぐ馬は有りませんでした。

＊たなばたの話は、彦星王子様と織姫様が１年に１度だけ７月７日に、天の川の岸で会うというものです。

To the readers,

These stories were written in 2011. That Spring, I was going to visit my mother (who was 95 years old) in Japan. But the Tohoku region which is just north of where my family lives received terrible earthquake damage. Also, so many people died from the resulting tsunami. I was very sad altogether. I decided not to go there at that time. In the past, my mother had always looked forward to seeing me as soon as she found out that I was coming to visit. It was a disappointment to both of us. I really wanted to do something for her. I was thinking about my childhood and how wonderful it was because of my parents' tender care. I started drawing these pictures and stories came to my mind while I was doing it, so I wrote them down. When I was done, I sent them to her which made me feel somewhat better. (I was able to visit her with my son and grandson the following year when things had settled down.)

That Fall, there was a writer's workshop in my area. I translated the stories from Japanese to English to share with my writer friends. They liked the stories and the pictures. They thought they were unique and that only I could have written them. My children and grandchildren liked them, too – especially my grandson who is in grade school. So I decided to call it "Grandma's Story" ("Obaachan no Hanashi" in Japanese).

I decided to share my stories with other children who might be interested in learning how Japanese country children lived in those days. It was more than a half century ago. Things have changed so much now, of course.

As my English writing has some flaws, I asked my son Jonathan to edit for me. Thanks to him, we went over the stories to correct my English mistakes.

I would also like to add thanks to my friends Jim and Mary Adams for safekeeping of my pictures and for burning them to CD-R for this publishing.

Sincerely,
Kou Lovin

- This book was translated, at times, according to my feelings--not word for word.
- Cover art was created by Chris Shepard. I made the paper dolls and put them in front of a Japan-like mountain and curved country road.

読者の皆さんへ

　　この物語集は、２０１１年に書かれました。その春、私は日本に住む９５歳になる母に会いに行く予定でした。ところが、私の家族の住んでいる（茨城県）すぐ北、東北地方が大地震の為に、大被害を受けました。そしてその後に来た津波の為に、何万という人達が亡くなりました。それらは、総て、本当に悲しいことでした。私はその年の旅をキャンセルすることにしました。過去に母は、私が又会いに来るよと知らせると、首を長くして待ち始めるのが常でした。そのキャンセレーションは、母と私にとって、とても残念なことでした。それで私は、彼女の為に何かをしてあげたいと頭をめぐらしました。両親の暖かい世話に包まれて育った幼い頃を思いました。その結果、それらの出来事を描き出し、描いているうちに色々なことが脳裏に浮かんで来ました。それが、物語の様に次々と出て来たので、それらを書き留めました。清書した後、その絵と文を母に送った時は、会えなかったとは言え、少しはましな感じがしました。（次の年に、地震が少なくなり、関東地方も少し落ち着いた頃、私は息子と孫息子、３人一緒に彼女を訪問することが出来ました。）

　　その秋、文を書く事の好きな人達の集まりが、この地方で催しされました。私はこの物語を日本語から英語に訳して、その人達に見せました。皆絵と物語が良いと言ってくれました。それらは個性の有る独特な物で、（もちろん）私にしか出来ない物とまで言ってくれました。私の子供達、孫達、特に小学生の孫息子が、おばあちゃんの話として興味を示して楽しんでくれた為、これを"おばあちゃんの話"と題付けることにしました。

　　そして私は、この楽しみを他の子供達にも分けることに決めました。日本の（特に田舎の）子供達が、ずうっと前毎日の生活をどの様に過ごしたかを知りたい人達もいるでしょう。もう半世紀も前の事だから、もちろん、今はずいぶん変わったけれども。

　　私の英語はちょっとした誤りが多い為、息子のジョナセン君に修正を頼みました。彼のおかげで、スカイプを通して２人で、正しい英語の使い方に修正することが出来ました。

　　又、良き友達ジムとメアリーアダムスさん達、私の描いた絵を、早いうちからコンピューターに入れて大事にしまっておいてくれ、今回の出版にコンパクトデスクに作ってくれた為、使うことが出来た事を深く感謝しています。

真実に
こう　ラビン

- この本の訳は、時には言葉ひとつひとつの訳でなくて、全体の"感じ"でしました
- 表紙の絵は、アーテストのクリスシェパード氏の日本的な山々とくねった道の前に、私が切り作った着せ替え人形の子供達を並べた物です。